# DISCOVER THROUGH CRAFT

# CHINA & THE SHANG DYNASTY

**Jillian Powell**

## FRANKLIN WATTS
### LONDON • SYDNEY

Franklin Watts
First published in Great Britain in 2016 by
The Watts Publishing Group

Series editor: Amy Stephenson
Series designer: Jeni Child
Crafts: Rita Storey
Craft photography: Tudor Photography
Picture researcher: Diana Morris

Picture credits:
Antracit/Shutterstock: 6-7 bg. Martha Avery/Asian Art & Archeaology/Corbis
via Getty Images: 12c, 15tr, 18b, 23b. Babel Stone/cc Wikimedia: 26c. Jurante
Buiviena/Shutterstock: 14-15 bg. James Burke/Life/Getty Images: 24bl.
catchasnap/Shutterstock: 18t. China Images/Alamy: 20t. G. D'Agli Orti/Getty
Images: 15cl. De Agostini/Getty Images: 32b. drs2biz/cc Wikimedia: 22-23bg.
Editor at Large/cc Wikimedia: 16b. Mary Evans PL/Alamy: 14t. Mauro Fabbro/
Shutterstock: 4t. Granger NYC/Alamy: 24tr. HIP/Alamy: 11b. Brian Holihan:
6b. Jeep2499/Shutterstock: 26-27bg. Jakrit Jiraratwaro/Shutterstock: 10b.
Chatchawai Kittirojana/Shutterstock: 7tlb. Lex art/Shutterstock: 7tl. Yan Liao/
Alamy: 23t. Ma Liu/cc Wikimedia: 1, 5t, Lou-Foto/Alamy: 11tr. MFB: 16c
mountain/cc Wikimedia: front cover bg, 19t. Pericles of Athens/cc Wikimedia:
7cl. Pictures from History/Bridgeman Images: 30b. Qin0377/Dreamstime: 4b.
Rosemania/cc Wikimedia: 12tl. The Saleroom: 8bl. Science Museum/Wellcome
Images: 27t. Chatchai Somwat/Shutterstock: 18-19 bg. Keren Su/Getty Images:
16t. Artur Synenko/Shutterstock: 11tc. tak wing: 6t. T & L/Getty Images: 14b.
WHA/Alamy: 20b. nik wheeler/Alamy: 22c. cc Wikimedia: 7br, 8tr, 10t, 26b, 28t,
28b. Monthira Yodtiwong/Shutterstock: 27c. Jiang Zhongyan/Shutterstock: 10-11bg.

HB ISBN: 978 1 4451 5081 9
PB ISBN: 978 1 4451 5082 6

Printed in China.

MIX
Paper from
responsible sources
FSC® C104740
www.fsc.org

Franklin Watts
An imprint of
Hachette Children's Group
Part of The Watts Publishing Group
Carmelite House
50 Victoria Embankment
London EC4Y 0DZ

An Hachette UK company

www.hachette.co.uk
www.franklinwatts.co.uk

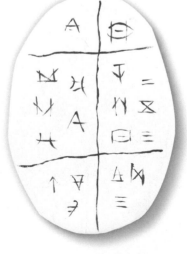

# CONTENTS

Words in **bold** can be found in the glossary on page 30.

Some of the projects in this book require scissors, paint, spray paint, glue, a needle, a hole punch and the sharp point of a compass. We would recommend that children are supervised by an adult when using these things.

# ABOUT THE SHANG DYNASTY

**The Shang Dynasty ruled part of China over 3,500 years ago, during the time of the Chinese Bronze Age. At the same time in ancient Greece, other Bronze Age civilisations were also appearing.**

Shang

This map shows the area of China ruled by the Shang Dynasty.

## Who were the Shang?

The Shang began as a **tribe** living along the Yellow River. King Tang of the Shang **overthrew** another king to rule the lands of the North China Plain, between the Yellow River and the Yangtze River (today this is called Henan Province). The king and his relatives were the highest social class. They formed a **government**, ruling over the army, priests, **merchants**, farmers, craftspeople and slaves.

The Yellow River gets its name from the colour of the mud that flows along it.

# When did they rule?

Thirty Shang kings ruled for over 600 years from around 1600 to 1046 BCE, moving their capital city several times. The king was the political and religious leader or 'high priest'. Shang people believed that the king was chosen by the gods, and could seek the gods' blessing and advice.

The people paid the king **taxes** and provided men for his army to fight other tribes or invaders from other lands.

King Tang was the first Shang ruler. This painting of him was made about 3,000 years after his death. He died in 1646 BCE.

# Shang skills

The first known written records in China date from the Shang Dynasty. The Shang were also the first Chinese people to be skilled at making and working **bronze**, as well as wood, pottery, **jade**, silk and leather. They were experts in hunting and fishing, but they also began to settle as farmers, growing crops and keeping animals.

## Quick *FACTS*

- the Shang ruled for over 600 years
- they used an early form of Chinese writing
- they were skilled in making bronze
- we know about the Shang from objects they left behind

## QUIZ TIME!

Which natural border protected the Shang from invaders from the east?

**a. the Gobi Desert**     **b. the Himalaya Mountains**     **c. the Yellow Sea**

Answer on page 32.

# DAILY LIFE

## During the Shang Dynasty, the rich lived very different lives from the poor.

This painting of Yin, the last Shang capital city, shows the style of buildings of the time.

## Cities and villages

Some Shang people lived in grand walled cities. The cities had high, thick walls made of earth, which was piled up and **rammed** with wood or stone to make it strong. Tall watchtowers made it easier to look out for enemies. Higher social classes, such as the king, priests and warriors, lived inside the walls. The king's palace would have been built high on an earth mound or platform in the centre of the city. The working classes, mostly peasant farmers, lived outside the walls in small villages.

This reconstructed rammed earth wall is in Zhengzhou – another of the Shang Dynasty's ancient capital cities.

# Buildings and homes

Grand buildings, such as palaces and temples, were built using the 'wattle and daub' method. This means wooden panels made from twigs and branches were plastered with mud or clay mixed with straw. Roofs were **thatched** with reeds. Inside, buildings were decorated with beautiful carvings, and silk **tapestries**.

Around the palaces and temples were rows of simple, rectangular buildings where craftspeople lived and had their workshops. In the countryside, people lived in caves or in houses dug into hillsides. Fire pits in the centre kept homes warm.

In summer, farm workers moved to bamboo or wooden huts in the fields to look after animals and crops. Some huts may have been raised on stilts or built as tree houses to keep people away from snakes and other wild creatures.

Wattle and daub

Reed thatch

Silk tapestry

This reconstruction of a Shang palace or temple in Yinxu houses a museum.

### HAVE A GO
Try making a model wattle and daub wall. Take four strong sticks and push them into a slab of clay, a few centimetres apart, to make a frame. Weave thin, bendy twigs between them. Pat wet clay onto the twigs to fill the gaps and leave to dry.

**?** Did rich and poor people wear the same clothes? Turn the page to find out.

# Chinese suit

The Shang designed the traditional Chinese suit, known as the *Hanfu*. The rich wore **embroidered** silk garments and hats and shoes made from leather and silk. The poor could only afford clothes made from plant materials, such as hemp, and simple straw sandals.

The earliest surviving embroidered Chinese silk dates back to the Shang Dynasty. Only the king was allowed to wear silk with dragon designs.

A Hanfu is a knee-length tunic with cuffs, a wide sash belt and a narrow, ankle-length skirt. Both men and women wore Hanfu.

# Silkworms

Silk comes from the **cocoon** of the silkworm caterpillar. A cocoon is made from a single silk thread, up to 900 metres long. Silk was so valuable to the Shang it was used as **currency**.

## QUIZ TIME!

What do silkworms feed on?

**a. bamboo**
**b. mulberry leaves**
**c. hemp**

Answer on page 32.

# Hair and jewellery

Hair was shaped into rolls, buns, topknots and pigtails, using hoops, combs and hair pins made from bone, jade, gold and copper.

These Shang fish pendants are made of jade.

## Quick FACTS

• men and women wore tunics called Hanfu
• Shang people were skilled at weaving and embroidery
• they kept silkworms for silk production

# Make this

Jade was a sign of nobility and was also believed to have magical and protective powers. It was carved into animal shapes, such as birds and fish, to make earrings and pendants. Make your own pendant from cardboard to wear yourself or give as a gift.

Jade has been a popular material in China for thousands of years and through all the dynasties. Today it is still used to make many beautiful and valuable objects. Jade can range in colour from creamy white to emerald green. It can even be orange, pink or brown!

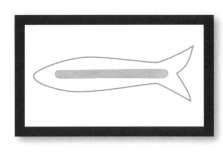

**1** Place a lolly stick onto thin, white card. Draw a fish shape around the lolly stick as shown.

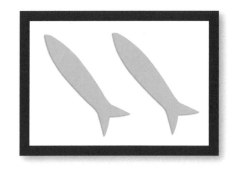

**2** Cut out the fish shape, then use it as a template to make another fish shape. Cut out the second fish shape. Paint them both a jade green colour.

**3** When dry, use a ballpoint pen to draw scales and fins on one fish shape. Glue the shapes together on either side of the lolly stick.

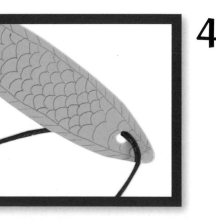

**4** Use a hole puncher to make a hole in the fish's head. You'll need to press hard to make it go through the stick. Thread a leather bootlace through the hole to complete your jade fish pendant.

# WORK AND WEALTH

**Most Shang people were peasant farmers, but people also worked as merchants, miners and craftspeople.**

## Hunting, farming and fishing

The Shang were skilled at hunting deer and other **game**; they fished in rivers and lakes – sometimes from simple boats – and they gathered wild foods, such as nuts and berries.

Peasant farmers worked small plots of land using stone and wood tools. Crops such as wheat and barley were grown. Farmers dug canals to carry water from the rivers to water their crops and they dug ditches to drain floodwater away. They kept animals including sheep, water buffalo and pigs.

This drawing shows a peasant farmer using a simple plough pulled by a water buffalo.

The Yangtze River is still used today to water the crops in farmers' fields along its riverbanks.

# Miners and merchants

Hundreds of men mined the copper and tin needed to make bronze. **Charcoal** makers turned wood into charcoal, which was then burned in the fires used to make bronze. Merchants traded in metals and salt, and they used cowrie shells as money. Coins were also cast from bronze in the shape of shells, spades, knives and bells.

Cowrie shells (above) – the shell of a type of sea snail – and this bronze spade (right) are two examples of Shang money.

## QUIZ TIME!

How were cowrie shells harvested from the Indian and Pacific oceans?

**a. using fishing nets**     **b. using coconut leaf mats**     **c. using straw baskets**

Answer on page 32.

# Precious materials

Most of the objects the craftspeople made were for the king and his nobles. Jade, bone and ivory – sometimes **inlaid** with **turquoise** – were carved to decorate weapons, and to make jewellery (see pp. 8 and 9) and **figurines**. Jade is a very hard stone to carve. It was polished with sand to make it smooth and gleaming.

This jade tiger was probably made for a royal or noble person.

## HAVE A GO

See what it was like to be a Shang craftsperson. Find a small rock or stone and see if you can make it smooth and shiny with sandpaper. It's harder than it sounds! Make sure you ask an adult to help you, and wear gloves when you try this as the sandpaper and rock can be rough on your skin.

**?** What other craft skills did the Shang practise? Turn the page to find out.

Only Shang royalty were allowed to own white pottery objects like this.

## Pottery

Potters used clay to make coil pots, smoothing and shaping them with wooden paddles. They may have had simple potters' wheels and they used **kilns** for firing (baking clay until it is hard) and **glazing**. Brown glaze was used for everyday pots and white glaze for precious objects. The finest pottery was **porcelain**, which is made using kaolin clay.

## Bronze

Bronze was used to make many things, from cooking pots and mirrors to weapons and bells. Large pots on legs (called 'dings') sometimes contained bowls for steaming foods, but were also used for rituals (see pp. 18–19). A noble's rank in society was measured by the number of bronze dings that he owned.

Most dings were decorated with patterns or animals. This unusual ding has faces carved onto each side.

To make bronze objects, clay **moulds** were decorated with patterns using sharp tools and patterned discs. The mould was cut into sections, fired to harden it and then put back together again. Molten bronze was poured inside and when it was cold and hard the mould was broken open to reveal the bronze object.

## Quick FACTS

- most people worked on the land
- farmers practised irrigation and flood control
- other people worked in mining, charcoal making, trade and crafts
- cowrie shells were used as a form of money, along with bronze objects

# Make this

The ding was a vessel used for cooking or offering food to gods or **ancestors**. Round or rectangular in shape, they stood on three or four legs. Make your own huge ding from a cardboard box!

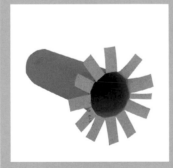

You can buy masks from art shops or you could look for pictures of other dings and copy the animal or swirling designs onto the cardboard instead.

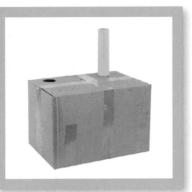

**1** Turn a large cardboard box upside down. Draw around a large cardboard tube at each corner, then cut out the circles.

**2** Tape cardboard handles, decorative shapes and masks to the sides of the box as shown.

**3** Make cuts 3 cm long and 1 cm apart at one end of each tube. (You will need four tubes.) Bend back the flaps.

**4** Slide the tubes through each hole on the inside of the box. Tape the flaps with duct tape.

**!** Ask an adult to help you use the spray paint.

**5** Paint the whole ding with brown paint. Leave to dry. Use gold spray paint all over the ding to give it a bronze effect. Leave to dry.

# WARFARE

**Shang kings could call up large armies to fight neighbouring tribes or invaders from other parts of Asia.**

This drawing shows Shang warriors on horseback attacking a fortress with rammed earth walls.

## Armies and warriors

Only the royal guard were professional warriors. Most soldiers were peasant farmers called up to fight for the king. They also did the hard work of building defensive walls and towers of rammed earth. The king could command an army of thousands, up to 13,000 for major battles. The cavalry rode horses and sometimes elephants. They fought alongside foot soldiers, and warriors in battle chariots.

## Prisoners

Success in war meant capturing prisoners of war – up to 30,000 at a time. Prisoners became slaves or were used as human sacrifices for the Shang gods and ancestors.

This Shang pottery statue shows a prisoner of war with his hands tied in front of him.

# Armour

Nobles wore body armour made from many overlapping pieces of shell or leather and bronze. Helmets were made from bronze, and thick pieces of leather stitched together, to make them strong enough to withstand blows from bronze weapons. Leather shields had bronze caps or blades that stuck out from the centre of the shield. The blades could be used to attack and defend in close combat.

This bronze helmet would have been very heavy to wear!

# Weapons

Weapons included swords, spears, knives, battle axes (see p. 16) and halberds (dagger-axes), which could reach up to 3 metres long. Bone, stone, wood, bronze and bamboo were all used for making weapons. Strips of bamboo were bent and then glued or tied together with silk to make bows. Arrows were made from bamboo or reed and had sharp, bronze tips.

Many Shang weapons, like this halberd blade, were carved and decorated with patterns or even scary faces (see p. 16).

## HAVE A GO
Try cutting squares of felt or fabric and stitching them together to strengthen them. See how many layers you need before it is impossible to pierce the felt or fabric with a needle. Think about how this would have helped protect warriors in battle.

**?** Which Chinese invention gave the Shang speed and power in battle? Turn the page to find out.

# Battle chariots

Warriors were led to battle by horse-drawn chariots made from wood with bronze fittings. They had huge spoked wheels measuring up to 1.5 metres in diameter and could travel great distances at speed, making them useful for patrolling land and borders to fight off invaders.

Two – or sometimes four – horses pulled each chariot. Each carried a crew of three. The charioteer (or driver) sat in the middle. On his right was a warrior carrying a halberd and on his left was an archer with a bow and arrows.

Chariots were often buried with royal or important military people who had died. Sometimes their horses were buried with them, too (see top right).

This bronze bird decoration was once fixed to a Shang chariot.

This bronze battle axe was carved with a scary face. It must have been a frightening sight for enemies of the Shang!

## Quick *FACTS*

- the army had divisions: royal guard, charioteers, cavalry and foot soldiers
- the Shang used a variety of weapons made from many different materials
- some Shang weapons were decorated with patterns or faces

## QUIZ TIME!

What else were chariots used for?

**a. carrying war supplies**       **b. war victory parades**       **c. royal hunts**

Answer on page 32.

# Make this

Shang axes like this one are called *yue*. To the Shang they were a **symbol** of power and authority. Make your own scary battle axe head to terrify your enemies. This one is much less deadly than a real bronze axe as it is only made of cardboard.

**1**

Copy the shape of the battle axe onto thick corrugated cardboard. Make the face as scary as you like! Cut it out. Ask an adult to help you cut out the holes in the middle.

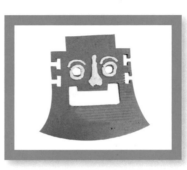

**2**

Paint PVA glue onto strips of kitchen paper. Roll them up and stick them on to form eyebrows and a nose shape. Leave to dry.

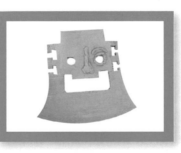

**3**

Paint both sides of the axe head with turquoise paint. Leave to dry.

You could hang your axe head on your bedroom door as a warning to 'keep out!'. Try attaching a short pole or stick to the short edge to make your axe even more realistic.

**4**

Dip a chunky paintbrush into brown paint. Dab off most of the excess paint onto kitchen roll. Gently dab the brush onto the axe head. Don't cover the whole axe head, just parts of it. This will make your axe look like old bronze. Leave to dry.

# RELIGION AND CEREMONY

**The Shang worshipped their ancestors and many gods, through prayer, ceremonies and offerings.**

## Shangdi

The ruler of all the gods was Shangdi. The king could ask him for advice, such as when to begin planting crops in the spring. The Shang also worshipped gods of nature, such as the Sun, wind, Earth, water and Moon.

The Shang believed Chinese dragons symbolised power and had control over water. Dragons are still an important part of Chinese culture today.

## Pleasing the ancestors

The Shang believed their ancestors could talk to the gods on their behalf to ask for health or a good harvest. To keep their ancestors happy, they performed ceremonies and offered gifts of food and wine. Temples and offering halls had large round or square altars made from earth. Animals and sometimes people were sacrificed to the gods on these altars as offerings to please the gods.

This elephant-shaped bronze vessel would have held wine and been used in religious ceremonies.

# Ritual vessels

Offerings of food, wine and water were made in ritual vessels made from pottery or bronze. They were made in the shape of animals (see picture on p. 18) and birds, and decorated with **geometric** or animal designs – or monster faces called *taotie*. Taotie faces were also used to decorate many dings. Some ritual dings were large enough to hold a person!

**HAVE A GO**
Try drawing a scary taotie face. Start by looking at some Shang taotie on the Internet or in books, then use your own imagination to design a beastly face that combines animal, human and fantastical features.

This large ding ritual vessel is decorated with a typical taotie design.

# Tombs

Tombs for dead nobles were dug from clay. The walls were lined with wood and decorated with paintings. Animals, servants and sometimes wives or soldiers were buried with their king or master. They may have been killed first or buried alive! The bodies of dogs, and slaves holding halberds, were placed around the corners of a tomb and in passages leading to it to guard the dead noble.

**QUIZ TIME!**
What happened to the bodies of peasants when they died?

a. **they were buried in pits or old wells**

b. **they were burned on fires**

c. **they were thrown in the Yellow River**

Answer on page 32.

**?** What kinds of objects were placed in royal tombs? Turn the page to find out.

## Queen Fu Hao

The Tomb of Queen Fu Hao was discovered in 1976 in the ruins of the Shang capital Yin. Queen Fu Hao was one of King Wu Ding's 60 wives and a powerful high priestess and leader in battle. She died in 1230 BCE. Among the tomb's contents were: 755 jade, 564 bone and 468 bronze objects, 6,900 cowrie shells, and the skeletons of six dogs and 16 slaves. Many of the objects were decorated with patterns and inscriptions.

Some of the many objects found in Queen Fu Hao's tomb.

## Grave goods

People believed that after death they went on to another life, so the rich were buried with objects they might need in the next life. Charms or **amulets** were buried with the dead to bring them luck and protect them from bad spirits. They were provided with everything they would need for the next life, including ritual vessels, weapons, jewellery and ornaments. Objects were made from typical Shang materials, such as bronze, pottery, bone, jade and silk.

A bi disc is a typical Shang charm. The shape is thought to represent the heavens or the sky.

## Quick FACTS

- the Shang believed that after death people went to an afterlife
- precious objects were buried with important people
- sometimes wives, servants and animals were buried with nobles

# Make this

Bi discs were magic charms to protect the dead and were usually made from carved jade. Make a bi disc and decorate it with Shang-style patterns.

**1** Take a ball of air-dry clay and roll it until it is about 5 mm thick. Use a pastry cutter about 10 cm wide to cut out a disc shape.

**2** Use a bottle top to cut out a circle of clay from the centre of the disc. Leave the clay to dry overnight or until it is hard.

**3** Paint the disc brown on both sides. Leave to dry.

**4** Using the point of a compass, scratch eight lines into the paint as shown.

> ! Ask an adult to help you and be very careful with the compass.

**5** In each of the eight sections, use the compass point to scratch Shang-style designs using straight and wavy lines. Repeat your design on the other side of the disc.

Some bi discs were made of glass instead of jade. The reverse side of the medals given to winning athletes at the 2008 Olympic Games in Beijing, China, were based on a bi disc design.

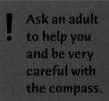

# MUSIC, DANCE AND ENTERTAINMENT

**During the Shang Dynasty, music and dance were used to celebrate the skills used in hunting and warfare.**

## Court entertainers

Musicians, mime artists, clowns, acrobats and dancers all provided entertainment for the king and his nobles. There were dances to celebrate royal hunts and many forms of dance were based on the movements of animals. They also put on plays in which 'face changing' actors used masks to represent different characters, such as gods, ancestors or spirits.

Experts think that masks like this bronze and gold one were carried on a pole during a performance.

### HAVE A GO
Try inventing a dance based on the movements of wild animals found in China. You could imitate the stealthy moves of a tiger hunting for prey, or the bendy action of an elephant's trunk as it seeks out leaves to eat or water to drink.

## Martial dance

Early forms of **martial** arts grew from the need to train men in the skills needed for self-defence, hunting wild animals and fighting enemies in times of war. Soldiers were given training in hand-to-hand combat and weapons' practice. Music and dance were used to build fighting spirit and martial skills. Martial dances were performed for public displays.

Martial artists today practise sword skills that Shang warriors would have been familiar with.

### QUIZ TIME!

Which martial art has its origins in China during the Shang Dynasty?

**a. taekwondo**

**b. judo**

**c. kung fu**

Answer on page 32.

This bronze sword blade is engraved with a leaf-like design.

**?** What kinds of musical instruments did the Shang play? Turn the page to find out.

# Musical instruments

Shang craftspeople made musical instruments from animal or bird bones, stones and bronze. Bells were cast from bronze and were struck rather than shaken. Bell casting was especially skilled work as the bell had to be **tuned** during the casting process. Bells were used to communicate with ancestor spirits and also to sound the retreat in battle, as well as to entertain.

Gongs and drums were made from wood, bronze and animal skins. Wind instruments included flutes made from animal or bird bones and the *xun*, a kind of 'flute' made from clay or bone, which was played by blowing into holes in its sides.

Like many Shang objects, this bronze bell is covered with beautiful patterns.

The holes in these xun make the instruments look like they have faces!

## Quick *FACTS*

- actors, musicians and acrobats entertained the king and his nobles
- actors used masks to represent different characters or emotions
- musical instruments were also used in religious ceremonies and in battle
- martial arts developed from training warriors

# Make this

A xun is one of the oldest types of Chinese wind instrument. It is often globe- or egg-shaped. Notes are played by blowing into the hole at the top and by covering and uncovering the holes in the side.

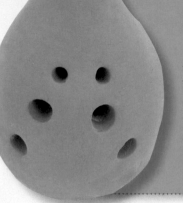

Experiment with blowing hard and blowing softly across the hole at the top. What works best? Make different sounds by covering and uncovering the holes. Can you make up a tune?

**1** Mould a ball of air-dry clay into an egg shape. Ask an adult to cut it in half as shown. Hollow out each half with a teaspoon.

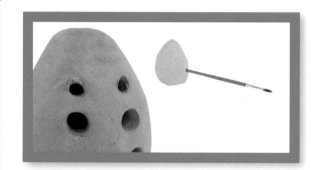

**2** Put the halves together, smoothing the join with your thumb. Make six holes in one side (and two on the opposite side close to the bottom) with the end of a paintbrush.

TIP: If you can't see the hole in the top, push the end of the paintbrush inside to open up the hole.

**3** Ask an adult to cut off the top. Leave the clay to dry overnight or until it is hard.

NOTE: These are the two holes on the reverse side of the xun.

**4** Paint the xun and leave it to dry.

# WRITING AND PROPHECIES

**An early form of writing was developed in China during the Shang Dynasty. Written history began in Britain around 1,000 years later with the arrival of the Romans in CE 43.**

## Chinese characters

The Shang is the first period in China known to have a written history. Simple characters were used to represent objects or ideas, a form of picture writing similar to ancient Egyptian **hieroglyphics**. Later, characters were used to represent individual words and sounds.

By about 1200 BCE there were more than 2,000 characters. They were painted with brushes and carved into jade, bronze, cattle bones and tortoise shells. They recorded agreements and payments, battles, weather, religious rituals and ceremonies.

## Modern characters

Some modern Chinese characters are clearly based on Shang script, such as the characters representing the Sun, a mountain or a farmed field.

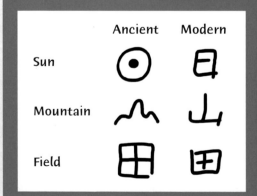

|  | Ancient | Modern |
|---|---|---|
| Sun | ⊙ | 日 |
| Mountain | ⌒ | 山 |
| Field | 田 | 田 |

Can you find the Chinese character for the Sun carved into the ox bone above?

# Calendar

The Shang observed the cycles of the Sun and Moon to create a calendar that had an accurate count of the days and months in a year. Cycles of 60 days were divided into ten-day weeks. Calendars were used to help plan farming and to predict events such as **solar eclipses**.

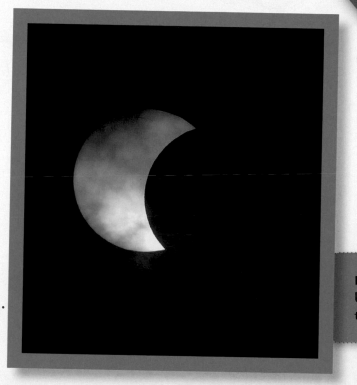

This Chinese calendar is based on cycles of the Moon. It is still used today to decide dates including Chinese New Year, which falls on the date of the first new Moon after 21 January.

For the Shang, a solar eclipse would have been seen as an event that was thought to bring either good or bad luck.

## QUIZ TIME!

The Shang believed a solar eclipse was caused by:

**a. the gods fighting**
**b. a dragon eating the Sun**
**c. dogs stealing the Sun**

Answer on page 32.

**?** How were marks made on shells and bones used to predict the future? Turn the page to find out.

## Oracle bones

The king used fortune tellers to ask his ancestors for advice and guidance. Oracle bones were flat ox bones (see p. 26) or turtle shells. A priest would carve the king's question onto the shell or bone, then heat a bronze pin and hold it against it until it cracked. A fortune teller would read the pattern of cracks to answer the questions.

This oracle bone is a turtle shell. The cracks and Chinese characters are clear to see.

This painting is of King Wu of Zhou, (Wuwang) the first Zhou Dynasty king.

## The dynasty ends

The Shang Dynasty lasted until around 1046 BCE, when slaves began to rebel against the king's cruelty and high taxes. The last Shang king, Di Xin, was overthrown by a rebel leader, Wuwang, who founded the Zhou Dynasty.

## Quick FACTS

- the Shang developed writing
- they used a form of picture writing, similar to hieroglyphics
- modern Chinese characters developed from Shang writing
- Shang fortune tellers cracked ox bones or turtle shells
- the Shang Dynasty ended in 1046 BCE and was followed by the Zhou Dynasty

# Make this

Oracle bones were used by the king's fortune tellers to predict the future. Make an oracle bone or shell for a Shang-inspired display and decorate it with Shang characters. (There is a link to a helpful website of Shang characters on page 31).

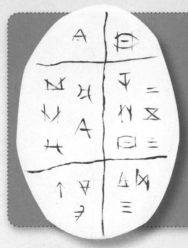

It would have taken a long time to make a real oracle bone. First, meat from the turtle shell was scraped away. Then the bone was polished to make a flat, smooth surface to carve the characters on.

**1** Cover a shallow oval dish with cling film.

**2** Cover with papier-maché, by pasting a mix of white glue and water onto strips of newspaper. Place them in overlapping layers over the cling film.

**3** Allow the papier maché to dry, then use the cling film to help pull it free of the dish. Paint it white and leave it to dry resting on the dish.

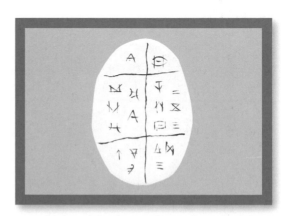

**4** Using black acrylic paint, divide the surface into six sections, and in each section paint Shang characters like the ones shown.

# GLOSSARY

**amulet** a lucky charm worn or carried to protect the wearer from evil or disease

**ancestors** relatives who died a long time ago

**BCE** 'before common era'; used for dates before the year 1

**bronze** a metal made from copper and tin

**Bronze Age** the period of history after the Stone Age when bronze was first used. The Chinese Bronze Age refers to the long period of history that began around 2000 BCE and lasted about 2,000 years

**charcoal** carbon that forms when wood is burned

**civilisations** advanced and cultured peoples

**cocoon** a silky case spun by some insects to protect the pupa inside

**currency** the type of money used in a country

**dynasty** a line of rulers where power is passed down to family members

**embroidery** patterns sewn with thread

**figurine** a statue of a human

**game** wild animals hunted for food or sport

**geometric** patterns made with lines and shapes, such as squares

**glaze** a material that colours pottery when it is baked in a kiln

**government** a group of people who govern a country and make laws

**hieroglyphics** writing that uses pictures or symbols

**inlay** a decoration where one material is placed inside another

**jade** a hard stone that that contains a mineral called jadeite

**kiln** a furnace for pottery

**martial** relating to fighting or war

**merchant** someone who buys and sells goods to make money

**mould** a container used to shape hot liquids as they cool and harden

**overthrow** to remove from power with force

**porcelain** a fine, white ceramic, sometimes called china

**rammed** earth that has been packed together tightly so it holds a shape, such as a wall

**solar eclipse** when part of the Sun is covered by the Moon as seen from Earth

**symbol** something that stands for something else

**tapestry** a thick fabric with woven designs

**taxes** a payment to a state or ruler that must be made

**thatch** a roof covering made of straw

**tribe** family groups or groups linked by location or culture

**tuned** adjusted so it makes a particular sound

**turquoise** a green or blue semi-precious stone

# BOOKS

***Daily Life of the Shang Dynasty*** by Lori Hile (Heinemann Educational)
***Great Civilisations: Shang Dynasty*** by Tracey Kelly (Franklin Watts)
***Great Empires: The Chinese Empire*** by Ellis Roxburgh (Wayland)
***Technology in the Ancient World: The Shang and other Chinese Dynasties***
by Charlie Samuels (Franklin Watts)
***The History Detective Investigates: The Shang Dynasty of Ancient China***
by Geoffrey Barker (Wayland)
***Collins Big Cat: The Shang Dynasty*** by Anna Claybourne (Collins Educational)

# PLACES TO VISIT

There are some Shang Dynasty objects that are in museum collections in the UK. There are many more museums of Shang artefacts in China.

***British Museum (London)***
***www.britishmuseum.org/***

***National Museum of Scotland***
***(Edinburgh) www.nms.ac.uk/***

If you are able to visit China, the National Museum of China has many objects from the country's ancient past, including Shang artefacts.

# WEBSITES

This site has lots of information about the Shang including family, religion and warfare.
**http://china.mrdonn.org/shang&chou.html**

This website has facts about the people and culture of the Shang Dynasty.
**http://www.historyforkids.org/learn/china/history/shang.html**

This site it packed with information, including a timeline, photo gallery, video clip and links to museum websites.
**http://www.thschoolrun.com/homework-help/shang-dynasty**

This website has a selection of Shang characters that appear on oracle bones.
**www.omniglot.com/chinese/jiaguwen.htm**

# INDEX

# QUIZ ANSWERS

**Page 5.** c – the Yellow Sea.
**Page 8.** b – mulberry leaves. The white mulberry tree is native to northern China.
**Page 11.** b – using coconut leaf mats. The mats were floated in the ocean and the sea snails would gather on them. The mats were then dragged onto the beach and the shells collected.
**Page 16.** a, b & c! Chariots were used for all of these things.
**Page 19.** a – peasants were buried in pits and old wells.
**Page 23.** c – kung fu is either a word for *all* unarmed Chinese martial arts, or it is a type of martial art similar to karate (which is Japanese).
**Page 27.** b – a dragon eating the Sun.